Forensic Artist: Solving the Case with A Face

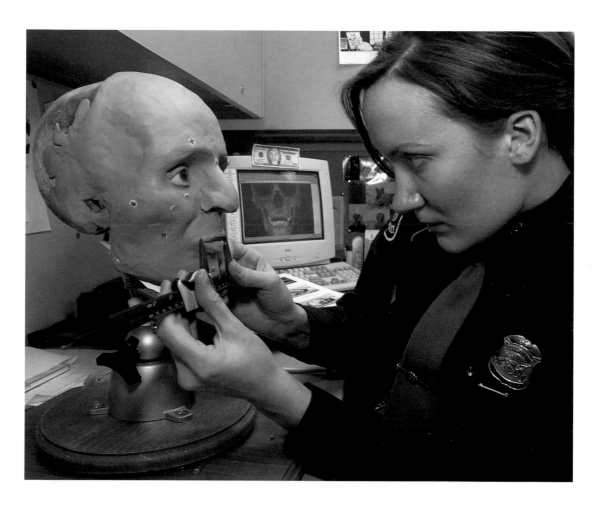

by Sue Hamilton

Published by ABDO Publishing Company, 8000 West 78th Street, Suite 310, Edina, Minnesota 55439.
Copyright ©2008 by Abdo Consulting Group, Inc. International copyrights reserved in all countries.
No part of this book may be reproduced in any form without written permission from the publisher.
ABDO & Daughters™ is a trademark and logo of ABDO Publishing Company.

Printed in the United States.

Editor: John Hamilton
Series Consultant: Scott Harr, J.D. Criminal Justice Dept Chair, Concordia University St. Paul
Graphic Design: Sue Hamilton
Cover Design: Neil Klinepier
Cover Illustration: iStockphoto
Interior Photos and Illustrations: p 1 Forensic artist, AP; p 3 Eye illustration, iStockphoto; p 4 Pencil, iStockphoto; p 5 Forensic artist, AP; p 6 Diameter tool, iStockphoto; Dr. Brown, courtesy John Bennett/Casebook: Jack the Ripper website; p 7 Wanted Poster, iStockphoto & Hamilton; p 8 Lizzie Borden, Corbis; Paintbrushes, iStockphoto; p 9 Bertillon card front & back, U.S. National Library of Medicine (NLM); Bertillon measurements-arm span, ear, hand, & foot, Library of Congress; p 10 Identi-Kit image, courtesy Paul Wright/Identi-Kit Solutions; Suspect sketch, AP; p 11 Pencil sketch of woman, iStockphoto; p 12 Identi-Kits & wanted poster, courtesy Paul Wright/Identi-Kit Solutions; p 13 Police officer with sketch of suspect, AP; p 14 Ryder truck axle from Oklahoma City bombing, AP; p 15 Timothy McVeigh & suspect sketch, AP; p 16 Image modifications of James Bulger, FBI; Jacob Wetterling images, National Center for Missing and Exploited Children; p 17 James Bulger images, AP; p 18 Brad Pitt images, AP; p 19 Surveillance image, AP; p 20 City sketch & notebook, iStockphoto; p 21 Artist Keith Alway, Corbis; p 22 Skull-on-photo, NLM/University of Glasgow; Police search, Univ. of Glasgow; p 23 Images of Buck & Isabella Ruxton, Mary Rogerson, Dr. Glaister, Jr., and police investigators, NLM/Univ. of Glasgow; p 24 Skull-on-photo of Isabella Ruxton and tiara & dress images, NLM/Univ. of Glasgow; p 25 Crowds at Ruxton's prison, Corbis; p 26 Skull, iStockphoto; p 27 Forensic artist at work (top & bottom), AP; p 28 Reconstruction and photograph of Shawn Patrick Raymond, AP; p 29 Hand-drawn skull, iStockphoto; Sketched reconstruction from woman's skull, AP; p 31 Reconstruction, AP.

Library of Congress Cataloging-in-Publication Data

Hamilton, Sue L., 1959-
    Forensic artist : solving the case with a face / Sue Hamilton.
        p. cm. -- (Crime scene investigation)
    Includes index.
    ISBN 978-1-59928-989-2
    1. Police artists--Juvenile literature. 2. Criminals--Identification--Juvenile literature. 3. Composite drawing--Juvenile literature. I. Title.
    HV8073.4.H36 2008
    363.25'8--dc22
                                        2007035159

CONTENTS

Artists in Law Enforcement

At first glance, art and law enforcement do not seem to go together. A crime scene investigator's job is to find evidence and clues to help figure out how a crime was committed and who was involved. How does a forensic artist fit in?

The word "forensic" means using science and technology to investigate crimes and provide facts in a court of law. Forensic artists add another dimension to this definition. Their work helps in capturing criminals, identifying victims, as well as aiding lawyers in court. They use their artistic skills in four major areas:

1) Composite Art – Creating pictures of a suspect based on descriptions provided by victims or witnesses.

2) Image Modification/Identification – Taking a photograph of a person and changing how that person looks. For example, a forensic artist can "age" the appearance of someone who disappeared years earlier to show what that person might look like today.

3) Demonstrative Evidence – Developing drawings or computer-generated artwork used in court to help present a case.

4) Postmortem (after-death) Reconstruction and Identification – Drawing or sculpting an unknown person's face from the decomposed remains found at a crime scene.

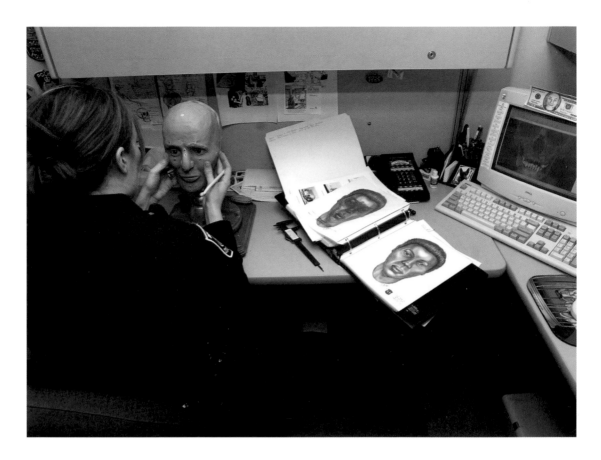

Blending creative talent with biology, anatomy, and anthropology, forensic artists are a unique part of crime scene investigations and courtroom cases. Their talents often provide crucial pieces of evidence that help solve cases. Their work may include hand-drawn or computer-generated illustrations, sculptures, photographs, or videos. Art may be two-dimensional (flat), three-dimensional, or even animated.

Whether producing a simple court case illustration or a complete facial reconstruction, a forensic artist's daily work is always different and challenging. States Richard Berry of the FBI's Investigative and Prosecutive Graphic Unit (IPGU), "The satisfaction is when our work is instrumental in helping to solve a case and bring a criminal to justice or bring closure to a victim's family."

Above: Trooper Sarah Foster, a Michigan State Police forensic artist works on a three-dimensional facial reconstruction from an unidentified human skull.

The History Of Forensic Art

Artists have used their talents in police stations and courtrooms for more than 125 years. In the late 19th century, England's Scotland Yard, the headquarters of the London Metropolitan Police, used artists to create illustrations of fugitives for "wanted posters." Lawmen of America's Wild West also hired artists to sketch pictures of such famous outlaws as Jesse James, Butch Cassidy, the Sundance Kid, and the Younger brothers. Many people studied the sketches, hoping to collect on the huge rewards offered for the capture of the criminals.

One of the first postmortem drawings was produced in London in 1888. On August 25 of that year, a brutal murderer began a 3-month killing spree that took the lives of at least 5, and possibly as many as 11, women. The killer was dubbed "Jack the Ripper" for the way he killed and mutilated his victims with a knife. Jack the Ripper's fourth victim was Catherine Eddowes. Dr. F. Gordon Brown, a pathologist, sketched Eddowes' body, showing the location and extent of the woman's wounds. Although Jack the Ripper was hunted for years, he was never found.

The case is studied even today. Based on police reports, as well as some details noted by Dr. Brown on his sketch, the killer was believed to have been left handed and probably had some medical knowledge.

Below: A sketch of pathologist, Dr. Frederick Gordon Brown.

Above: A mockup of an Old West wanted poster for the bank and train robber Jesse James.

Right: A drawing of a courtroom scene with Lizzie Borden and her lawyer, George Robinson. Publishers used artists' sketches of sensational court trials to help sell newspapers and magazines.

Newspapers soon employed the talents of law enforcement artists. In famous cases, sketches of the accused, as well as victims and witnesses, were published along with sensational newspaper-selling stories. In August 1892, 22-year-old Lizzie Borden was accused of killing her father and stepmother with a hatchet in their Massachusetts home. Courtroom drawings of Borden were printed in newspapers, along with gruesome details of the crime. The young woman was found not guilty.

Although selling newspapers may not have been the best use of forensic artists' talents, the media did help law enforcement, asking citizens to study sketches made of thieves, killers, and missing persons, and report any leads to their local police. This practice continues today.

In the 1880s, French criminologist and anthropologist Dr. Alphonse Bertillon developed a system to identify criminals. He created an ID sheet, known as "portrait parle" or "speaking likeness," that showed drawings or photographs of a criminal, as well as measurements of his or her face and body. At first, the ID sheets were used to identify and keep track of local criminals. Later, after many sheets were collected into a book, the pictures and descriptions of facial shapes, hair, eyes, ears, nose, chin, and so on were used to help victims and witnesses provide descriptions of perpetrators to an artist. Using the visual examples, the artist created a sketch that was given to police and newspapers. Many countries throughout Europe and North America began using Bertillon's system of identification. It was the start of what would grow into the composite work of a forensic artist.

Above: The front and back of a 1911 Bertillon card used to identify criminals.
Below: New York City Police take arm span, ear, hand size, and foot size measurements to fill out a 1908 Bertillon card.

Composite Art

Above: A composite image using Identi-Kit technology.
Below: A police sketch of an unidentified suspect taken from witness descriptions.

One of a forensic artist's most challenging, yet most fulfilling, tasks is creating composite art. The word composite means to be made up of various parts. For a forensic artist, this translates into taking witness descriptions of a criminal's head shape, hair style, forehead, eyes, nose, mouth, chin, ears, as well as any facial hair, glasses, scars, moles, or tattoos, then combining each of the parts into one image. The resulting composite art is turned over to investigators. Sometimes TV stations, newspapers, and magazines are also given the composite art so that the public can help find the perpetrator.

It is often difficult for a witness to give an artist an accurate description. Without looking, imagine trying to describe a friend's face. Most people are able to describe their friend's hair color (blond, brown, red, or black) and his or her hair style (long, short, curly, straight), but describing a friend's eyes, nose, mouth, and ears is much more difficult.

Now try to describe a classmate's parent, whom you may have seen for only a few moments. Maybe he or she dropped off homework or a forgotten lunch. Do you even remember the person's hair color and style? Often, witnesses see a criminal for only a few seconds. Rather than being in a relaxed and familiar place such as at school, witnesses are often in frightening, unfamiliar, and sometimes life-threatening situations. It is very difficult to stay calm enough to remember the details of a thief or attacker's face. Sometimes the perpetrator is even disguised, or wearing a ski mask or other head covering.

Above: A pencil sketch of an unidentified woman. It is often difficult for a witness, who may have only seen a criminal for a few moments, to provide an accurate description. However, a trained forensic artist may help witnesses remember facial details to create a good likeness.

Above: A collection of Identi-Kits from the early "box kits" with individual images on cards to the more modern software program used on today's computers.

Below: A sample of an Identi-Kit image and the captured suspect.

Composite artists were aided in their task in the 1950s with the production of the Identi-Kit. The first Identi-Kits were commonly referred to as "box kits." They came with foils—clear plastic sheets printed with different facial features. A witness was asked to pick out the correct facial shape from a selection of different foils. Then they would pick out hair, cheekbones, mouth, nose, ears, eyes, eyebrows, eyeglasses, and headgear. Each sheet was stacked one on top of the next, until a final composite image was created.

At first, foils were printed with hand-drawn features, similar to what an artist would have done. Later, the kits used photographs of real people's features. Today's Identi-Kit is a computer software program that creates composite sketches on the screen, which are then e-mailed, posted on websites, or printed out and distributed.

Some law enforcement agencies feel that hand-drawn art by a skilled forensic artist is the best choice when trying to come up with a composite sketch. An artist is able to ask questions and possibly help witnesses remember something they'd forgotten. Plus, an artist can make many different variations, depending on a witness' input.

Above: A police officer reviews a sketch of a suspect. Computer-generated images may be e-mailed, posted on websites, or printed out and distributed to the media.

On April 19, 1995, in Oklahoma City, Oklahoma, a yellow rental truck filled with 5,000 pounds (2,268 kg) of explosives blew up in front of the Alfred P. Murrah Federal Building. The disaster resulted in the deaths of 168 people, 19 of them children. It was a terrorist attack in the middle of America's heartland. Agents of the Federal Bureau of Investigation (FBI) were called in to help catch the perpetrators.

In searching the crime scene, a piece of the truck used to hold the bomb became an important clue. Although blown apart in the explosion, the truck's axle was found, upon which was printed the vehicle identification number, or VIN. By tracing the number, investigators were led to a Ryder Truck Rental company in Junction City, Kansas. Company records revealed that the man who rented the vehicle used the name Robert Kling. This proved to be an alias, or false name. However, eyewitnesses at the rental company provided FBI forensic artist Ray Rozycki with a good description of the man. Rozycki created a drawing, which was immediately shown throughout the area. A motel owner thought she recognized the person. She said it looked like a man named Timothy McVeigh, who had stayed at her

Below: A close-up of the rear axle of the rental truck used in the Oklahoma City bombing, and a part of the vehicle identification number (shown highlighted) that was assigned to the vehicle.

motel a few nights before the bombing. She even had his home address.

This was an important break. Investigators used their computer network to track McVeigh. To their surprise, they discovered that their suspect was already in jail. Only 90 minutes after the bombing, McVeigh had been stopped for driving his car without a license plate.

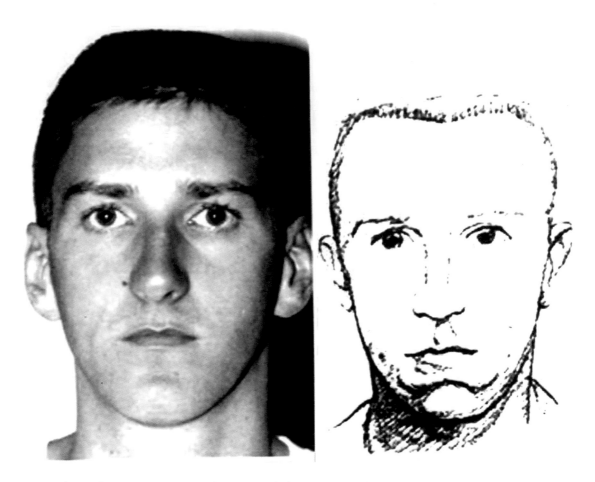

When the state trooper discovered that McVeigh was carrying a loaded gun, the 27-year-old was arrested and taken to the Noble County Jail in Perry, Oklahoma. On April 21, investigators put in a hurried call to the jail. McVeigh, who was waiting to go into court for carrying a concealed weapon, was returned to his jail cell and held until federal agents arrived.

Thanks to the work of crime scene investigators, as well as a talented forensic artist working with eyewitnesses, McVeigh was quickly found and arrested. The Oklahoma City bomber, as he came to be known, was tried in a court of law and found guilty. McVeigh received the death penalty, which was carried out on June 11, 2001.

Above: Timothy McVeigh, left, and the artist sketch of the bombing suspect that was released by the FBI the day after the bombing.

Image Modification

Above: Modified images of fugitive James Bulger created by the FBI.
Below: Jacob Wetterling, missing since 1989, shown at age 11 and age-progressed to age 29.

During a crime scene investigation, forensic artists may be asked to modify, or change, an image. For example, forensic artists may use their skills to "age" criminals or missing persons who have been sought for many years. However, this isn't as simple as adding wrinkles or subtracting hair. Different people age very differently. Even a single year can make a major difference in the appearance of a child. While adults usually have less dramatic changes from one year to the next, their looks do change—either accidentally or, in the case of some criminals, on purpose.

An artist must take into account such things as:

- Is the person male or female?
- What is their race? A person of European ancestry may age very differently from a person of African or Asian ancestry.
- How did the person's parents or grandparents look at this age?
- Does the person have any brothers or sisters? What do they look like?
- What was the person's lifestyle? Did he or she exercise? Eat right? Was the person very thin, or overweight?
- How was the person's health when last seen? Did the person smoke? Or take drugs? Did the person spend a lot of time outside?

Above Top: Organized crime fugitive James "Whitey" Bulger is shown in these 1984 images. *Above:* Image-modified photographs of Bulger, released by the FBI in 2002.

Above: At a glance, would you know these men are both famous actor Brad Pitt?

Artists use their knowledge of anatomy, as well as family history and scientific research, to help them produce these "fugitive updates" and "age progressions." Also, since criminals may purposely try to change their appearance, artists may be asked to change a suspect's appearance by producing images that show different hair styles, glasses, or facial hair. A man with shoulder-length hair and a full beard and mustache looks very different with a buzz cut and no facial hair.

But image modification does not stop there. Artists may also be asked to improve the quality of photos or videos that show fuzzy, blurred, or partial images of criminals, witnesses, or other people sought in an investigation. For example, security cameras often capture crimes in progress. Sometimes the videos or photos show unclear images. Perhaps the camera's lens was dirty or smudged, or maybe the tape or film was old, resulting in a poor-quality image. Maybe the person is in the shadows, or is only seen from the side. Forensic artists produce criminal sketches based on the partial images that can be seen. Artists may also work with other photographers or video technicians to produce the best possible images.

Above: A forensic artist may look at a fuzzy or blurred video image, such as this taken from a surveillance camera just before an attack on a security guard, and create a sketch of the criminal.

Demonstrative Evidence

The saying "a picture is worth a thousand words" helps describe what a forensic artist does when creating demonstrative evidence for a court case. Demonstrative evidence can be an actual object, or it can include pictures, models, videos, or other visual items created by a forensic artist to help show what happened during a crime.

It is often difficult for a victim or witness to describe what happened during a robbery. It is even more difficult for a judge and jury, who may never have been at the scene of the crime, to understand exactly what happened. A forensic artist's work can help. For example, in a bank robbery, a forensic artist may be asked to create a sketch or model showing where a robber entered the bank, which teller window he approached, where other people were standing, and how the robber exited the building. The artist might also be asked to create a timeline showing exactly what time each event occurred.

An artist may be asked to produce a simple sketch, or he or she may have to go to a crime scene and create a very detailed video. Whatever the task, the artist's job is to create visual evidence that makes a case more understandable in court.

Above: Artist Keith Alway illustrates a variety of subjects, in particular medical and legal illustrations, as seen displayed in a Ventura, California, courtroom.

Skull-to-Photo Forensic Technique

Above: A skull-to-photo illustration of murder victim Isabella Ruxton. *Right:* Police investigators undertake the gruesome task of searching for body parts in an area near Moffat, Scotland, in September 1935.

In 1935, a skull-to-photo photographic process was first used to identify an unknown murder victim in Great Britain. Body parts, including two skulls, were discovered under a bridge near Moffat, Scotland, on September 29, 1935. Some of the remains were wrapped in newspaper pages. Investigators determined that the newspaper came from a Sunday, September 15, special edition sent to homes in a specific part of the city of Lancaster, England. Police began questioning people in the area, and soon became suspicious of a local physician, Dr. Buck Ruxton. He had recently claimed that his wife, Isabella, had left him for another man. Both Isabella and the couple's maid, Mary Jane Rogerson, had disappeared, without a goodbye to anyone, on September 14.

Above, Left to Right: Dr. Buck Ruxton. Ruxton's wife, Isabella. Mary Jane Rogerson, the Ruxtons' maid. Dr. John Glaister, Jr., a forensic pathologist who worked on the Ruxton murder investigation.

Above: Police investigators walk with a bag of body parts found in an area near Moffat, Scotland, in September 1935. Because there were two victims, and the pathologists had to reconstruct the bodies from a number of jumbled body parts, the newspapers began calling the case the "Jigsaw Murders."

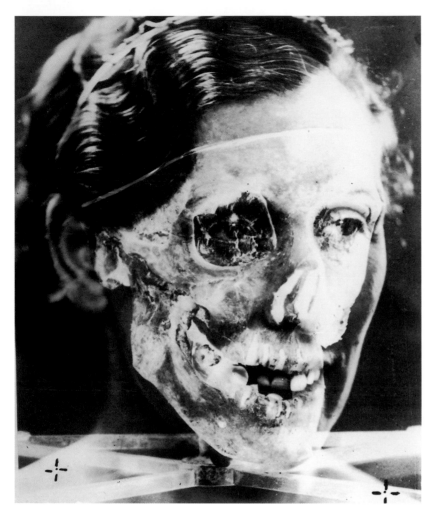

The two skulls were sent to the forensic team of Glaister, Smith, and Brash in Edinburgh, Scotland. John Glaister, Jr., and Sydney Smith were experienced professors of forensic medicine. James Couper Brash was a professor of anatomy. The team came up with the idea of taking a photo negative of one of the skulls and putting it on top of a photo of Isabella's face. By superimposing the two images together, they discovered a perfect match.

Above: In 1935, forensic scientists came up with the process of superimposing a photo on a skull. This shows a photo of Isabella Ruxton and a skull that was found in Moffat, Scotland. The match is exact. The process is still used today.

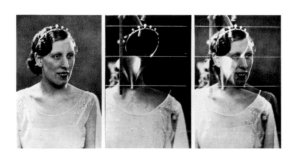

Left: Scientists compared the skull to several different photos of Isabella Ruxton. To be sure the image size was correct, the photographer took an existing photo, then photographed her tiara and dress, then superimposed the two images together.

Above: Police struggle to hold back crowds on May 12, 1936, the day Buck Ruxton was hanged for the murder and dismembering of his wife and their maid.

This new forensic technique was one piece of evidence that resulted in the arrest, trial, and conviction of Dr. Ruxton. He later confessed to murdering his wife in a jealous rage. He strangled the maid to keep her from telling the police. Ruxton was hanged for his crimes on May 12, 1936. Skull-to-photo comparisons are still used today.

Postmortem Reconstruction

Above: Using a skull and whatever clues were found with it, such as clothing or hair, a forensic artist tries to recreate a face, hoping that someone will be able to identify the person.

In postmortem reconstruction, modern science and art combine to help identify people that have been dead so long that only their bones remain. This is sometimes accomplished by creating clay sculptures of long-dead faces.

To begin, forensic scientists study the corpse's other bones to give them clues to the unknown person's sex, age, ethnicity, and size. If the skull is the only bone available, then forensics experts must come up with their "best guess" answers. They decide if the skull belonged to a young or old man, woman, or child, and if that person was of a small, normal, or large size. They determine whether the person's race was based on European, African, or Asian ancestry.

Armed with these conclusions, forensic artists work alone or with forensic anthropologists to recreate facial features. These forensic scientists use their knowledge of human anatomy and how people live to develop images of what people may have looked like. Artists may create flat, two-dimensional drawings or three-dimensional facial sculptures right on the skull.

The first step in reconstructing a face is to place tissue depth points on the skull. Precise tissue depth charts give the thickness of muscle, fat, skin, and other tissue for males and females of different body sizes and ancestries. For example, a thin Asian man would normally have less tissue depth than a heavy European woman.

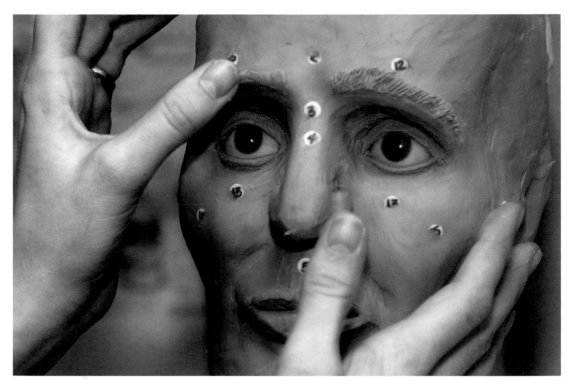

Above and Below: A forensic artist works on sculpting a face on a skull.

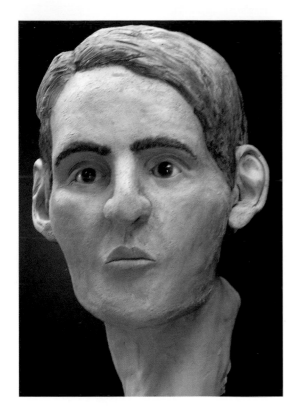

Forensic artists use depth markers made from vinyl eraser strips, which are cut to varying lengths for different parts of the face. These depth markers, which look like pencil erasers, are then glued in their proper place on the skull. The artist now has a guide for creating the shape of the face.

For a two-dimensional drawing, the skull is photographed with the tissue depth markers in place. A flat, life-sized print is then made. A piece of paper is placed over the photograph, and the artist begins the work of drawing the person's facial features.

In a three-dimensional recreation, artists use clay to sculpt the face. They begin by covering the skull with clay until it is as thick as the tissue depth markers. Plastic eyes are placed in the center of the eye sockets, and the detail work of sculpting the facial features begins. If teeth are still in the skull, artists will sculpt the mouth to show a smile. This is a facial feature that witnesses often see and sometimes recognize. Otherwise, the mouth is sculpted in a closed position.

Left: A skull reconstruction created in 2004 helped investigators identify a man, Shawn Patrick Raymond, who had been missing since 1983.

Sometimes forensic artists and anthropologists have other clues to work with. Even a few strands of hair help artists recreate a person's correct hair color and length. Skin color may be deduced from tissue fragments found on the corpse. However, if there are no other clues, artists work on the face based on the skull's shape.

Measurements taken at various points on the skull help form the face. For example, the widest point of the hole in the skull over which the nose rests (the nasal aperture) tells forensic artists how wide to make a person's nose. Another part of that same area, the anterior nasal spine, helps artists decide where to place the tip of the nose.

Once completed, the drawing or sculpture is given to investigators, who often release the artwork to the media to see if anyone recognizes the person. Many victims have been identified thanks to the skills of forensic artists and anthropologists. Their work helps solve some very mysterious cases, and provides investigators with opportunities to bring criminals to justice.

Right: A drawing made from an unidentified woman's skull.

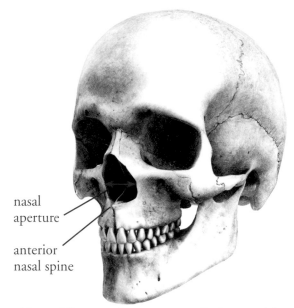

nasal
aperture

anterior
nasal spine

Above: The nasal aperture tells how wide to form a nose. The anterior nasal spine shows where to place the tip of the nose.

GLOSSARY

ANATOMY — The study of the bodily structure of humans, animals, or plants.

ANIMATED ART — Pictures or diagrams that are made up of a number of different images, all shown in rapid succession one after the other.

ANTHROPOLOGIST — A person who studies all areas of human life including their origins, history, behavior, speech, religion, as well as their physical, social, and cultural development.

CORPSE — A dead body.

CRIMINOLOGIST — A person who studies crimes and criminals to understand how these people think and behave. A criminologist's work helps law enforcement find and capture criminals by predicting what a criminal may do in certain situations.

DECOMPOSE — A process that happens after death when a body begins to rot, breaking down into its most basic elements.

EVIDENCE — Objects, and sometimes information, that helps prove the details and facts in a legal investigation.

FBI — The Federal Bureau of Investigation is a division of the United States Justice Department responsible for enforcing federal laws.

FUGITIVE — A person who runs away from the law.

MUTILATE — Badly injured, often violently.

NASAL APERTURE — The opening in the skull over which the nose rests.

PATHOLOGIST — A person who studies diseases and how they affect human bodies at different stages.

PERPETRATOR — A person who commits a crime.

POSTMORTEM — After death.

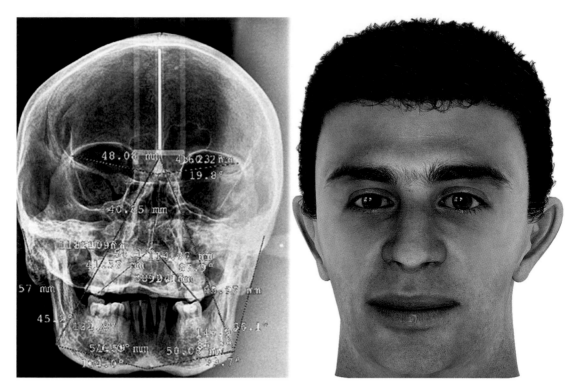

Above: A reconstructed face created using modern computer technology. The skull belonged to a resident from ancient Pompeii, a city near Naples, Italy. The man was killed during a volcanic eruption of Mount Vesuvius in 79 A.D.

THREE-DIMENSIONAL ART — Art, such as a sculpture, that displays an object's three dimensions: length (from front to back), width (from side to side), and depth (top to bottom).

TIMELINE — A series of events shown in the order they happened. A timeline may be shown with only words or only pictures, but often is a combination of both.

TWO-DIMENSIONAL ART — Art drawn on a flat surface such as a pencil illustration on a piece of paper. The drawing shows length and width of an object.

VIN — Vehicle Identification Number. A set of letters and numbers given by manufacturers to every vehicle produced in their factory. Each vehicle has its own unique VIN. When a vehicle is sold, licensed, or insured, the VIN is used to identify the vehicle.

INDEX